This roadmap is not about making money.

♦

It is about keeping money.

First edition.

ISBN: 978-0-9985252-7-3

Disclaimer

I am not an attorney, CPA, or financial advisor, and nothing in this manual constitutes legal, financial, tax, or investment advice.

What follows is MY ROADMAP — the framework I designed for my own situation, my own family, and my own goals. It is provided as a reference only so that you can see one practical, real-world example and use it to help you construct, with the guidance of qualified professionals, YOUR ROADMAP.

There are countless reasons you should not simply take my plan and plug your life into it. Your citizenship may be different. Your tax environment may be different. Your personal goals, family dynamics, risk profile, assets, and age are almost certainly different from mine.

Laws change. Service providers evolve. Wealth levels vary. And at my age, my priorities are not likely to match yours.

This manual is my plan — the structure that helps me navigate complexity, protect my family, remain organized, and sleep at night. It will continue to evolve as I move through the phases, make new decisions, and adapt to changes in law, technology, family needs, and global conditions.

We are conditioned to think that now that you have money, you invest it, live on the proceeds, pay your taxes, give some away, and when you die whatever is left gets passed out to your heirs.

That can work, but there is a better way.

In simple terms, you can create a ***Wealth Management Structure*** *(like a "company") that invests your pot of gold so that it generates profits. Those profits are paid out to the heirs like dividends. You run it like a company and pass it on from generation to generation.*

> *This is what rich folks do. This is how the rich stay rich. Now that you have a pot of gold, you can do the same.*

This Roadmap shows you how that system works. I won't tell you it is simple, but you were smart enough to get that pot of gold, you can do this!

This roadmap will show you how you can build a team of professionals that will do the heavy lifting under your supervision, while you sip a margarita on a beach somewhere.

Using This Roadmap

If one day you needed to drive from Barstow California to Bangor Maine, and you did not have GPS or a roadmap, you would find the trip challenging to say the least. You would be stopping frequently to ask for directions, constantly trying to avoid wrong turns, trying to figure out where you went wrong, and how to get back on track. It would be an arduous journey and probably more than a little intimidating.

You currently face a similar situation. You have come into a sizable "pot of gold" and you are asking the same questions … where am I going and how do I get there?

This book is a roadmap. It is not a GPS. A fair analogy would be comparing Google Maps to the GPS on your smartphone. With Google Maps you can see the overall scope of the trip; that nice blue line as it crosses each state. With that understanding, you can customize your trip so you can visit your aunt in Casper Wyoming. It gives you a big picture. However, it does not give you real-time turn-by-turn directions. It is not looking over your shoulder telling you when you missed an exit, where the next gas station is, or how you get back on track when you are lost.

As you would with Google Maps, use this Roadmap to understand the big picture; then use your advisory team as your GPS to give you the turn-by-turn instructions. **Together is where the magic happens.**

Note From The Author

As I said, I am not in any way a financial adviser. I'm eighty-one and long retired, my career was as an engineer and international businessman.

I came into wealth late in life and found myself faced with the same challenges you might be facing at this time. My engineer's brain kicked in: *I need a systematic approach*.

My response was to study and design a plan to solve my problem. This roadmap, or more accurately an early version, was the result. As I lived it and corrected my many mistakes, I realized that others that find themselves in a similar situation could benefit from my efforts and experience. This book is the result.

Imagine we meet at Starbucks. I talk; you listen. By that I mean read this book cover to cover. This is not the time to challenge or dig in, stay high-level, just absorb the landscape.

Now go to your office or kitchen table and grab a notepad or your computer and read it again. Dig in. Go Phase by Phase. Take notes. Make adjustments. Tag the important things. Prioritize.

This is how you start developing your own roadmap. Work your way through Phases 1-3. You can do this on your own. Once you have, you are ready to reach out; that starts in Phase 4.

I hope you benefit from this material, and I hope it helps you to relax and enjoy the process.

TJG

This Manual Is For

This manual is intended for anyone facing new or sudden wealth, complex circumstances, family-protection concerns, a need to develop an understanding of the HNW or UHNW financial management landscape, or long-term planning challenges.

It is intended for those who:

- *Want a high-level, practical reference point rather than vague theory.*
- *Need a simplified framework to organize professionals, tasks, phases, and priorities.*
- *Want to avoid the classic failure modes: disorganization, procrastination, compliance errors, family conflict, and other avoidable risks.*
- *Prefer to understand the "why" behind the roadmap before handing it to their attorney or FO (Family Office) director to formalize.*
- *It specifically addresses these two broad (liquid assets) categories:*
    - *High-Net-Worth Individuals (HNWI): roughly $1M–$25M*
    - *Ultra-High-Net-Worth Individuals (UHNWI): $25M+*

My Personal Goal:

<u>Become invisible, bulletproof, and able to sleep at night!</u>

Your goals may differ. You will work on that in Phase 3.

Wealth Tier Framework

This manual uses a Tier-based framework to discuss planning, governance, and structural considerations. These Tiers don't specifically align with the "official" definition of HNW and UHNW individuals, but the granularity makes it more relevant to specific actions outlined in this book. The values shown are conceptual and intended to provide scale context rather than precise financial classification.

Tier	Net Worth Range	Conceptual Meaning
Tier 4	<$5,000,000	Foundational wealth; limit structural complexity
Tier 3	$5,000,000 – $25,000,000	Early HNW; planning is increasingly important
Tier 2	$25,000,000 – $50,000,000	Established HNW; formal structures advisable
Tier 1	$50,000,000 – $100,000,000	Significant wealth; governance and privacy critical
Tier 1+	>$100,000,000	Ultra-HNW; institutional-grade planning required

If your pot of gold is below $15,000,000, you may find the overhead required to implement the full structure outlined here to be detrimental to your overall goals. However, even in those circumstances, don't skip this manual. Phases: 1, 2, 3, & 5 and the Appendices are the same, and critical no matter the size of your pot. The conversations you have and the professionals you engage may differ slightly, but they still need to happen. Most of the Appendices are equally critical regardless of Tier level.

As your wealth grows, the more advanced concepts will become relevant. Early familiarity provides a roadmap to grow into, and it allows you to have better conversations with professionals, ask sharper questions, and avoid costly mistakes.

Just a reminder, this is a roadmap, not a GPS; it will not identify every challenge, but it will give you the tools and mental models to recognize the common traps and to build a stable, private, long-term structure around whatever level of wealth you manage.

Bring this manual to your professionals. Let them critique it, modify it, and translate it into legally appropriate structures for your jurisdiction and circumstances. It is a guide, not a plan; use it to stay organized, informed, and in control as you move through each phase

— it is not a substitute for qualified professional advice.

Contents

Phase 1: Silence

Goal

Stay silent about your wealth-event.

Tell no one — not family, not friends, not coworkers. Not "just one person." Job #1 is to keep your mouth shut until you are fully protected.

Reason

- *Talking exposes you.*
- *People you trust will leak information—always.*
- *Not because they are bad, but because humans cannot keep life-changing secrets.*
- *Once news spreads, you cannot pull it back.*
- *You become a target for guilt, jealousy, pressure, scams, threats, and manipulation.*

Silence keeps control in your hands. Talking hands control to others.

Actions

- *Say nothing about the money, the amount, or where it came from.*
- *If someone notices you acting differently, deny everything.*
- *If you feel the urge to talk, write the urge down on paper and burn it.*
- *Keep normal routines. No sudden changes.*
- *If contacted by anyone involved in the event (bank, broker, etc.), take notes and keep conversations short and factual.*

  - *Be careful! There are so many ways to con you. These are just a voice on a phone. They may not be who they say they are.*
- *If someone asks questions you aren't ready to answer, use this phrase:* ***"I have some personal matters I'm sorting out. Nothing to talk about."***

Do Not

- *Do not tell your best friend.*
- *Do not celebrate. Do not hint. Do not "joke."*
- *Do not tell your boyfriend / girlfriend.*
- *Do not tell children, siblings, parents, extended family.*
- *Do not tell neighbors, coworkers, church members, or anyone you know socially.*
- *Do not text, email, or post anything connected to the event.*
- *Do not ask anyone you know for advice or referrals.*
- *Do not search for professional help using your normal email or phone.*
- *Do not change your lifestyle. No new cars, no new clothes, no sudden generosity.*
- *Do not make promises to anyone.*
- *Do not "do something nice" to relieve guilt. That opens the door to demands.*

Phase 1 Ends When

You meet all the following conditions:

1. You have not told a single person about your wealth event.
2. You have not hinted or suggested anything to anyone.
3. No one around you suspects anything.
4. You feel calm enough to make decisions slowly.

5. You understand that talking will harm your future, your safety, and your family.
6. You are ready to move into Phase 2 without breaking silence.

If you messed up and told someone, it will make future phases more difficult, and it could risk your safety and security. Stop talking and move to Phase 2.

Phase 2: Lockdown

Goal

Secure your information, identity, and documents before anyone realizes you have something worth taking.

Your job is to close every easy door a criminal, scammer, or "helpful" person could walk through.

Reason

In the early days, your biggest risk is not losing money—it's **losing control**.

People can dig into your life using your devices, your email, your mail, your trash, your social media, and your habits.

If your information leaks, professionals' hands get tied, and your problems multiply.

You cannot recover a breached identity.

Actions

- *Gather all documents related to the wealth event (papers, emails, notices).*
- *Make two copies of everything. One digital. One physical.*
- *Store originals in a safe place inside your home.*
- *Store one backup in a second private location (not a bank, not a friend's house).*
- *Create a new, clean email used only for your future professional team.*
    - *Do not include your real name.*
    - *Do not reuse old passwords.*
- *Create a new, clean (paper) notebook for logging every decision, date, and contact.*

- *Freeze your credit with all major credit bureaus.*
    - *In the U.S. the three major credit bureaus are: Equifax, Experian, and TransUnion*
    - *It is free, but you must request a freeze from each bureau individually. You can do this online, by phone, or by mail—online is the fastest method.*
- *Turn on two-factor authentication for your critical accounts.*
- *Check your mail daily. Remove anything with personal or financial data immediately.*
- *Shut down all social media posting.*
- *Reduce your digital footprint:*
    - *Delete or lock down old accounts.*
    - *Remove personal information from public "people finder" sites.*
- *Use only your normal daily routines. No unusual purchases.*

Do Not

- *Do not trust cloud storage with sensitive documents.*
- *Do not take photos of documents with your phone.*
- *Do not use your normal email or phone for anything related to the wealth event.*
    - *Purchase a "burner" phone*
- *Do not discuss your new phone, email or notebook with anyone.*
- *Do not put documents in a bank safe deposit box (not yet).*
- *Do not announce changes in habits, passwords, or accounts.*
- *Do not throw away paperwork without shredding it.*
- *Do not use public Wi-Fi for anything related to your situation.*

- *Do not sign anything.*
- *Do not call an attorney or CPA yet.*

Phase 2 Ends When

You meet all the following conditions:

1. All documents are organized, copied, and safely stored.
2. You have a clean, private phone and email dedicated only to Phase 3 and beyond.
3. Your credit is frozen.
4. Your online footprint is reduced.
5. Your accounts are locked down.
6. No one knows you are doing any of this.
7. You feel confident that your information and identity are secure.
8. You can proceed without exposing yourself or leaving traces.

Finish any incomplete items before moving to Phase 3.

Phase 3: Goal Setting

This is the key to building your wealth management system and your new life.

Read through this entire roadmap before you define your goals. Doing this will help you to understand your options and some of the different approaches which could lead to different conclusions. A simple example is how you define your heirs. You will also have difficulty if you do not understand what generational wealth is and how you organize to take advantage of this powerful system.

Goal

Sit alone (or with spouse if appropriate) and determine what kind of life you want to build.

Define your destination before you hire anyone to build the path.

Reason

Without a clear understanding of your goal, you will not be able to maintain control of the process.

If you don't set the target, someone else will — a lawyer, a CPA, a relative, a salesperson, or a charity.

Confusion leads to waste, regret, and conflict—especially between spouses.

You cannot hit a target you haven't identified.

Actions

- *Go to a quiet room. No TV. No phone. No interruptions.*
- *Write down what you want your life to look like in 5, 10, and 20 years.*

- *If married, your spouse must complete this exercise separately first.*
- *Compare answers. Talk calmly. Find agreement or compromise.*
- *Choose your general **lifestyle category:***
    - ***Quiet Comfort:** modest improvements (home upgrades, reliable car, travel 1–2×/year).*
    - ***Enhanced Lifestyle:** bigger travel, better home, more freedom, high-quality experiences.*
    - ***Multiple Homes / High Travel:** seasonal living, extended cruises, long trips abroad.*
    - ***Generational Wealth:** protect and grow your wealth for children / grandchildren.*
    - ***Full Simplicity:** low profile, privacy-first, minimal lifestyle changes.*

Write Down

- *Your desired lifestyle category*
- *Your non-negotiables*
- *Your "absolutely nots"*
- *Put this page in your Phase 2 notebook.*
- *Commit to reviewing it once per quarter.*

Do Not

- *Do not talk to anyone else about your goals.*
- *Do not compare yourself to others.*
- *Do not assume your spouse "knows" what you want.*
- *Do not aim for extremes (reckless indulgence or monk-level minimalism).*
- *Do not allow guilt or fear to shape your decisions.*
- *Do not let early emotions steer you.*

Phase 3 Ends When

You meet all the following conditions:

1. You have a written, specific vision of your future lifestyle.
2. If married, you and your spouse have reached agreement.
3. Your goals are realistic for the level of wealth involved.
4. You understand that **this vision will guide every decision in future phases.**
5. You can articulate your goals clearly and calmly without apologizing or justifying.
6. You are ready to engage professionals without letting them steer your life.

If any item is missing, you remain in Phase 3 until it is resolved.

There should be no wiggle room here, no *"I will do it later"*, complete it now, it is critical.

3A: The Charity Trap

Most people who come into sudden wealth immediately think:

- *"I should give back."*
- *"I should help others."*
- *"This is my chance to do good."*

This instinct is normal — but **it can be Dangerous**

Acting too early can create long-term complications that are difficult to unwind.

Why This Happens

Humans are conditioned to trust:

- *Big charities*
- *Familiar names*
- *Medical causes*
- *Cute slogans*
- *Heart-tugging stories*
- *Social pressure*
- *Family needs*
- *Church guilt*

Those instincts are natural.

Reality

What follows is **my personal view based on observation and experience.**

Not all charities are efficient, and not all are corrupt. Most people working inside nonprofit organizations are sincere and well-intentioned. However, large, well-known charities can sometimes operate in ways that would surprise you.

Some:

- *Spend heavily on administration and fundraising*
- *Focus more on visibility than measurable outcomes*
- *Maintain long-term problem narratives rather than solving root causes*
- *Develop sophisticated donor cultivation systems*
- *Actively pursue individuals who appear capable of making substantial gifts*

New wealth attracts attention. Even without announcing it, your financial behavior can signal capacity.

My position is simple

Before you donate meaningful money, you must verify how an organization operates, how it allocates funds, who controls decision-making, and whether its results align with your expectations.

Giving without investigation may feel generous, but it can introduce unnecessary risk.

A Practical Way to Think About It

Think of charitable giving as "impact investing".

You are allocating capital with the expectation of producing a real-world outcome.

If an organization has existed for decades, some more than a century, and the core problem remains largely unchanged, it is reasonable to ask:

- *Is the organization solving the issue*
  … or managing it?
- *Are incentives aligned with resolution*
  … or with continuation?

These are not accusations — they are due diligence questions.

I am not suggesting that you distrust charities.

I am suggesting that you verify them.

My Recommendation

Wait until you have completed Phase 8 and your structural protections are fully operational. At that point, you can design philanthropic efforts that reflect your values, are properly vetted, and do not commit resources to organizations or causes that are not aligned with your goals.

Your Thinking May Change

Wealth changes everything. It offers the luxury of a broader view. I am not saying that your charity of choice is bad, or that you will alter your giving, but you might. Set the money aside if you wish, but don't execute until you have reorganized your life around your newfound wealth.

This is the same logic I applied when I waited to buy a new car. For me, the car I would have purchased initially was not the car I selected a few months later. Still a new car, just a different car.

Phase 4: Contact Professionals

Goal

Identify and speak with a small group of qualified, experienced, big-city professionals—without exposing yourself, your money, or your identity.

Reason

You cannot manage sudden wealth alone. But the wrong lawyer or accountant can cost you far more than poor investments or avoidable taxes.

Many professionals will confidently claim they understand complex wealth events. In reality, if they are not both deeply experienced and current with evolving laws and structures, the consequences can undermine your protection and long-term success.

When possible, prioritize firms located in major metropolitan financial centers where professionals are more likely to have routine exposure to high-net-worth clients, liquidity events, and complex cross-jurisdiction structures.

You want to find the right people without tipping your hand.

I strongly advise you to review this entire book before you contact anyone. It will help you understand what questions to ask and what their responses mean. You can learn "on the fly", but you will learn more and get better answers if the person you are talking with senses that you have done your homework. You do not need to be an expert, but understanding concepts and terminology will prove beneficial. It might also help you avoid costly mistakes or select the wrong person to work with.

Actions

- *Use your clean Phase 2 phone and email (and nothing else) for all research and contact.*
    - *Clean phone and email is important because there are "reverse lookups" tools that could expose your identity and location before you wish for that to be known.*
- *Target major city law firms and CPAs. Firms in larger metropolitan areas often have more exposure to complex wealth events.*
- *Look for professionals who specifically mention:*
    - *"High-net-worth clients"*
    - *"Liquidity events"*
    - *"Complex estates"*
    - *"Asset protection"*
- *Make a list of 5–7 candidates in each category (attorney / CPA).*
- *Contact them using your clean phone or email and say:*

"I need to speak with someone experienced in handling significant private financial matters. I prefer a short introductory call."

- *Keep every message short, unemotional, and generic.*
- *During calls, take notes in your Phase 2 notebook.*
- *Ask direct screening questions:*
    - *"How many high-net-worth clients do you handle?"*
    - *"How many clients with sudden wealth or liquidity events have you worked with?"*
    - *"What is your typical first-week protocol?"*
    - *"Do you coordinate with private banking or security services?"*
- *Stay calm. Let them talk.*
- *End every call the same way:*

"Thank you. I am interviewing several professionals. I will get back to you."

You are looking for skills and experience, but also someone with a compatible personality and to some extent age range. If you are 70, you will probably feel less comfortable with someone who is 30. The reverse is also true. It is not prejudice; it is just human nature.

Do Not

- *Do not contact any professional using your normal email or phone.*
- *Do not tell them amounts, sources, or details yet.*
  - *Firms may have lower limits … ask.*
  - *Do not give financial specifics, <u>talk broad ranges only</u>.*
- *Do not hire anyone during the first call.*
- *Do not tell them your family situation.*
  - *They will key on whatever you divulge, so be careful what you tell them.*
- *Do not let them rush you.*
- *Do not use any professional who:*
  - *Talks more than they listen.*
  - *Claims "this is simple" or "I handle everything."*
  - *Has no recent experience with wealthy clients.*
  - *Works in a small town or small firm.*
  - *Seems too eager or pushy.*
- *Do not discuss this phase with anyone you know.*
  - *You do not want referrals from friends or family.*

Phase 4 Ends When

You meet all the following conditions:

1. You have spoken with at least 3 real attorneys and 3 real CPAs from major cities.
2. You have eliminated anyone weak, inexperienced, or talkative.
3. You have identified 2–3 serious candidates in each category.
4. You have told none of them the full picture yet.
5. You feel calm, in control, and under no pressure.
6. You are ready to make appointments to choose your core team without rushing.

Phase 5: Temporary Money

Goal

Protect your assets.

Reason

You are now building a protective structure around you. But until the long-term plan is fully in place, you need a simple, safe way to hold and use money without creating chaos, waste, or exposure.

This is not about investing.

This is not about celebrating.

This is about parking money safely and preventing self-inflicted wounds.

Action

Create a temporary plan that protects you for the next 3–12 months while the big-picture strategy takes shape.

Step 1 — Park the Bulk of the Money in "Sleep Well" Assets

Until your legal, tax, and estate structures are complete, place the majority of your funds into simple, boring, non-volatile holdings:

- *FDIC / NCUA-insured accounts (spread across banks if necessary)*
- *U.S. Treasury bills (3–12 months)*
- *High-quality money market funds (Treasury-backed only)*
- *Short-term CDs*

These are not investments. They are temporary parking spaces while you and your advisors catch up.

Create a Temporary Budget (3–12 Months)

Rule

No lifestyle upgrades for 90 days.

Almost all catastrophic wealth failures come from blowing money before the plan exists.

After that 90-day period, you may:

- *Upgrade essentials (housing, transportation, debt payoff)*
- *Improve family support responsibly*
- *Start cautiously improving quality of life*

You must avoid "permanent lifestyle creep" until the long-term plan (Phase 6) is built.

Controlled Spending System

Set up **three** temporary accounts:

Operations Account

Your daily spending and monthly bills.

Fund with 3–6 months of your normal expenses.

Opportunities & Emergencies Account

For unpredictable needs.

Fund with 6–12 months of expenses.

Major Purchases Account

For anything over $10k.

Enforce a **72-hour waiting rule** before spending. This slows you down just enough to avoid emotional buying but not enough to annoy you.

Debt Cleanup (Be Smart About It)

Good to eliminate now:

- *Credit cards*
- *High-interest personal loans*
- *Car loans*
- *Small lingering debts you "forgot about"*

Wait on these until Phase 9:

- *Paying off mortgages*
- *Paying off family members' debts*
- *Don't co-signing anything*
- *Buying real estate as gifts or "helping someone out"*

Use your professional team to guide you. They have been through this before and they know where the traps are. The wrong debt payoff at the wrong time can mess up taxes, relationships, and legal protections.

Freeze Lifestyle Expansion (Temporary)

Wealth shock triggers powerful emotions.

Your brain will push you toward:

- *Buying something to "feel normal"*
- *Over-gifting*
- *Upgrading everything*
- *Solving everyone's problems*
- *Playing the hero*

For 90 days:

- *No new cars.*
- *No new homes.*
- *No "just helping someone real quick."*

If you violate this rule, the entire roadmap becomes harder to stabilize. Rely on your team's for guidance.

Temporary Giving Plan (So You Don't Get Burned)

Family and friends will want help.

You may want to help.

But gifts are emotionally dangerous early on.

Use this approach

1. Create a "90-Day Freeze."
   No gifts, loans, or bailouts.
2. Create a Separate "Giving List."
   When someone asks for money, say:

   > **"I'm in a temporary freeze. Write down what you need and I'll review it later."**

3. Evaluate after Phase 8 (Long-Term Design).
   This protects them, protects you, and prevents rushed emotional decisions.

Repeating this Family Rule

Family support is opportunity support, not an ATM.

That means

- *Education support*
- *Business startup support (only with a business plan)*
- *Healthcare support*
- *Emergency support*
- *Structured, rule-based help*

Not

- *"Can you help me buy a car?"*
- *"I need help with rent again."*

- *"I want $50k to open a cupcake store."*
- *"Can you pay for my wedding?"*

If you hand out money freely, your wealth and your freedom ends in

- *Dependency*
- *Envy*
- *Family conflict*
- *Lawsuits*
- *Ruined relationships*

People value opportunity.

People resent handouts.

Sorry, but this distinction needs to be repeated multiple times in the book.

Cash Withdrawal & Carry Rules

You're temporarily high-risk for:

- *Theft*
- *Fraud*
- *Manipulation*
- *Sudden generosity*
- *Emotional overspending*

Rules

- *Never carry more than $300 cash*
- *Never withdraw more than $2,000 without logging it*
- *Never hand out cash without **a mandatory 24-hour pause***

Emotion fades quickly.

Regret lasts a lot longer.

Phase 5 Ends When

- *Money is safely parked and not at risk of emotional decisions*
- *Your basic 3-account system is running*
- *You have 3–12 months of low-volatility parked assets*
- *You have stopped lifestyle changes for at least 90 days*
- *No major gifts or loans*
- *You can breathe without feeling pressure to "do something" with the money*

Outcome of This Phase

You should be stable, calm, and mentally clear.

You avoid the #1 cause of sudden-wealth disasters: **rushing.**

Your money is protected from the world—and from yourself—while you build the permanent system.

Phase 6: Structural Elements

Important Context Before We Proceed

This is where we identify the types of structures and organizations that will hold your assets and manage your investments. Think of it as if you are having initial discussions with your architect. In Phase 3 you established your long-term goal. In Phase 4 you selected a team to help operate your "company". In this phase you are learning what the various organizations are, what each one does, how they differ, and where they could fit within your Wealth Management Structure that will be established in Phase 7.

Let me start at the destination and work back. Remember my goal is to be invisible, bulletproof, and thus able to sleep at night. Let me break that down as this is the Phase is where the magic happens.

You won't live long if you sit on your front porch with a pot of gold. Even in the safest neighborhood, someone will come after it. So, you have to hide it … invisible. Even if you hide it behind the shed, you still need to lock it in a safe … bulletproof. But you still want to enjoy the benefits of your gold, so it has to be accessible in some fashion. In my case, my advisors constructed a multilayer safe hiding place. An irrevocable trust in the Cook Islands (CIT), a set of LLCs under the CIT in Nevis, and additional trusts and domestic LLCs. Almost all of my assets went into

CIT and were distributed down through the various LLCs and trusts.

Wait a minute! You gave all of your money away? Well yes and no! Let's start with a definition:

Legal Fiction
A "legal fiction" is a false assumption accepted by the law as true to enable legal rules to operate or be applied in a practical, fair, or consistent way, even though the assumption is not factually accurate.

So, I gave away the money but not the control. You are probably thinking that still seems a bit shaky. But I will tell you that I was already using a basic level of this legal fiction without even knowing it. So are you. Let me explain. I have bank accounts, my home is in a trust, and I have an LLC for a rental property. I did this on my attorney's advice. Here is what that actually means:

The rental is in an LLC because as the name implies, it limits my liability. If someone trips on a hose at the property and sues me, my personal assets are shielded because I don't actually own the rental property, the LLC owns it. My home is in a trust to avoid probate. When I die, it simply passes on to the person or persons I have designated. Yes, I can do this in a will, but then things like probate and taxes kick in. I won't go down that rabbit hole but trust me you want to avoid probate if possible. The trust makes that possible.

Now this may come as a surprise, but when you put your money in a bank, it is no longer your money. It belongs to the bank. What you get in return is basically an IOU that allows you to demand the bank return a portion of your money or pay bills with online banking. You probably have a debit card to make that easy. Think about the alternative, walking around with a pocket full of cash and handing out cash whenever you want to pay a bill. That would be annoying, and it would also make you an easy target for robbery.

So, you see, at a rudimentary level, I was already taking steps to make myself invisible, bulletproof, and able to sleep at night. What we are planning here is to take that to a whole different level. The process is complicated, but thousands of people have already done it and that is what your advisors are here to do for you.

What follows reflects the elements of my personal structure based on recommendations from my advisory team.

The tone is intentionally direct because my advisors were very specific about how my structure should be organized, and what I should avoid. You don't want fuzzy logic here. These are critical decisions and I suggest that you want your advisors to be as blunt with you.

Jurisdictions, laws, and political climates shift. Regulatory enforcement intensifies or relaxes. What is considered optimal for my situation, my priorities, and my risk tolerance, at this specific point in time, may not be appropriate for your situation.

Therefore, before implementing any international structure, you must work with qualified legal, tax, and compliance professionals who understand your situation, your jurisdiction and the current global regulatory environment.

Tax Avoidance

Let me make this very clear, none of this is about tax avoidance. You do not want to do that. Your team will work to legally minimize your taxes, but if anyone tries to avoid taxes, fire them immediately.

Revocable vs. Irrevocable Trust — It Matters

Revocable Trust = Convenience + Probate Avoidance

- *You still legally own the assets.*
- *A judge can order you to hand them over.*
- *Creditors, ex-spouses, lawsuits, or the government can reach them.*
- *This is NOT true asset protection.*
- *Excellent for estate planning, terrible for protection.*

Irrevocable Trust = True Asset Protection

- *You do not legally own the assets anymore.*
- *A judge can issue orders — but legally you no longer control the assets.*
- *Lawsuits hit a wall.*
- *Divorce lawyers hit a wall.*
- *Creditors hit a wall.*
- *Predatory family members hit a wall.*

If someone wants bulletproof safety, the controlling trust MUST be irrevocable.

The only downside?

You must be comfortable with giving up nominal ownership in exchange for absolute protection.

Why the TOP TRUST Should Be IRREVOCABLE

Because

- *If a court can force you to revoke it, change it, or access it … it is not protection.*
- *If you retain ownership, the assets are considered "yours" … they are attackable.*
- *If you want cross-border protection (U.S. court orders become meaningless), it MUST be irrevocable.*
- *If you want to block future political shifts, tax grabs, or legal changes, irrevocable is the only safe option.*

This is why nearly ALL serious asset-protection attorneys insist on an irrevocable offshore trust at the top.

The Serious Offshore Jurisdictions

There are multiple jurisdictions that your advisors may recommend. I chose the following for the reasons listed.

Cook Islands Trust (CIT)

- *Gold standard for decades*
- *Zero recognition of foreign judgments*
- *One of the strongest legal protection frameworks available*
- *Shortest statute of limitations to attack transfers*
- *Trustees known to resist U.S. pressure successfully*
- *Used by Fortune 500 CEOs and Ultra-HNW families*

I am told that this is one of the most robust asset-protection jurisdictions available.

Nevis

- *Often paired with Cook Islands*
- *Excellent LLC laws*
- *Asset transfer attacks require bond posting (extremely expensive for attackers)*
- *Fast action: injunctions and freezes require local court appearances — killers for foreign litigators*
- *Strong protection, slightly more flexible than Cook Islands*

Think of Nevis as the "operational muscle" below a Cook Islands trust.

The Specific Structure (This is the Real Muscle)

Here is the structure we implemented:

Cook Islands Irrevocable Trust

Role

The **vault** — the true owner of the wealth.

What goes in:

- *Ownership of Nevis LLCs*
- *Ownership of holding companies*
- *Sometimes ownership of offshore bank accounts*
- *Sometimes ownership of certain IP or securities*

What does not go in

- *Daily-use assets (house, car, etc.)*

These sit in domestic LLCs below it.

Nevis LLC(s)

Role

The operational layer under the trust.

Typical uses

- *Hold brokerage accounts*
- *Hold offshore bank accounts*
- *Act as the "active entity"*
- *Own domestic LLC(s) beneath it*

Offshore Private Bank

Role

The financial engine.

Options

We have all heard of private banks in countries like Switzerland, Liechtenstein, and Singapore. There are other jurisdictions that may be appropriate. Your advisors will guide you based on your circumstances.

For personal security and privacy, I do not disclose my specific banking selections.

Domestic LLC(s)

Offshore LLCs (Nevis in my case) are not appropriate for all assets. Assets tied to your daily U.S. life are more commonly placed in a Domestic LLC owned by your Offshore LLC. This could include things like your house, your vehicles, investment real estate, and your operating businesses. The selection has to do with estate planning, probate, and taxes. The State the LLC is organized in can also be important. Your advisors will recommend the correct configuration and location based on your circumstances.

Summary

These structural elements are where my advisory team accomplished my goal; **invisible and bullet proof allowing me to sleep at night.**

Phase 6 Ends When

This Phase never really ends. These structures are representative of what I would expect your advisors to organize for you.

Reread this Phase multiple times until you feel comfortable with the various elements and how they relate with each other.

When you work with your advisor, it may be helpful to have him/her relate their recommendations to the information in this Phase. That will help you understand your structure and ensure that major elements are not missing.

You may also find the information in this Phase useful when working with your heirs.

Phase 7: Building Your Infrastructure

> *This phase determines whether your wealth becomes*
> ***secure, invisible, and long-lasting***
> *or fragile and exposed.*

Revisiting the roadmap analogy, this is where Google Maps joins with GPS. You are now working with your team to design a structure that is appropriate for your goals and your Tier level.

Goal

To create your **multi-layered, internationally resilient protection system** using best-in-class jurisdictions and entities (*structural elements*).

Introducing (Onboarding) **Your Family**

The question of when and how to involve family members is both personal and complicated.
It is addressed separately in Phase 7A below.

Reason

This Is Where Your Wealth Becomes Organized, Invested, and Protected

… And Where Your Team Takes On The Heavy Lifting

You are using the structural elements to assemble the engine room that will power the rest of your life:

- *Banking*
- *Custody*
- *Investment infrastructure*
- *Trusts*

- *Asset protection structures*
- *Tax systems*
- *Reporting and compliance*

Your advisor team will manage all the above

Actions

The Minimum Core Components:

- *One domestic private banking relationship*
- *One or more offshore private banking relationships*
- *Proper custody accounts*
- *Trusts and legal entities*
- *A tax strategy that fits your jurisdiction*
- *A unified reporting system*
- *A vetted team of advisors (CPA, attorney, fiduciary, banker)*

Each piece must support the others. You are building a system, not a collection of random accounts.

The Advisor Map (Who Does What and Why They Matter):

- ***CPA:*** *tax strategy and compliance*
- ***Estate Attorney:*** *trusts, entities, and protection*
- ***Private Bankers*** *(Onshore + Offshore): custody, lending, execution*
- ***Investment Fiduciary:*** *portfolio design, risk management*
- ***Asset Protection Attorney:*** *international structures*
- ***Insurance Specialist:*** *risk transfer, liability buffers*

No single advisor can do all of this. You want redundancy and specialization, do not rely on one guru. This team may well form the core of your Family Office. *See Appendix D*

Designing Your Private Banking Architecture

"AUM" (Assets Under Management)

You will hear this term a lot. AUM is the amount of your money a bank or advisor directly manages or custodies. AUM matters because service levels, access, and influence scale with your AUM at that institution. The magic threshold for world-class service is roughly $50MM per bank.

Primary Domestic Private Banks: JPM, Citi, Morgan Stanley, BofA, Wells Fargo

Ideal for

- *Daily liquidity*
- *U.S. investments*
- *Domestic credit lines*
- *Bill pay*
- *Trust integration*

Not ideal for

- *Privacy*
- *Asset protection*
- *Global diversification*
- *Litigation insulation*

Offshore Private Banks: Switzerland, Singapore, Liechtenstein, Luxembourg, Cayman

NOTE: Certain trust structures, particularly those established in offshore jurisdictions, may require banking relationships aligned with that jurisdiction. This is typically coordinated by legal and fiduciary advisors.

Ideal for

- *Long-term preservation*
- *Confidentiality (legal and compliance)*
- *Multi-currency holdings*
- *Geopolitical diversification*
- *Superior custody*

Not ideal for:

- *Basic daily use*
- *U.S.-specific tax structures*
- *Simplicity*

Domestic banks handle life.

Offshore banks protect wealth.

Why a Single-Bank Strategy Is Dangerous Above Tier 3

At higher wealth levels, keeping everything in one bank — especially in one jurisdiction — creates unacceptable risks:

- *One subpoena*
- *One lawsuit*
- *One cyber event*
- *One bank policy change*
- *One jurisdictional disruption*
- *One relationship manager leaving*

Could compromise your entire financial life.

The Multi–Private Bank Model (Typically Used by Tier 1 & Tier 1+)

Once you exceed Tier 3, the global norm: **multiple banks + multiple jurisdictions**.

This eliminates single-point failures, creates competition between banks, and provides geopolitical diversification.

Sample Allocation Models by Tier

Net Worth	Domestic PB	Offshore PB #1	Offshore PB #2	Optional Tier 3
Tier 3 & Tier 4	80–90%	10–20%	—	—
Tier 2	10–20%	30–50%	20–30%	Maybe
Tier 1	5–15%	40–50%	40–50%	Optional
Tier 1+	minimal	30–40%	30–40%	20–30%

Phase 7 Ends When

You have implemented and funded your banking strategy developed with your financial team.

Do not move to Phase 7A or Phase 8 until your banking structure has been implemented and your wealth secured.

7A: Family Onboarding

This is where things get personal, complicated, and occasionally messy. In all likelihood, this will be the most challenging part of building your structure.

Before you start, you should have already established your goals in Phase 3 and completed Phase 7. If you have not completed that work, put this section aside and finish those phases first. Without clear goals, family onboarding becomes reactive instead of intentional, and without establishing your structure, you will find yourself pulled in multiple directions; this is not a good place to operate from.

It is impossible for me to provide a clean, universal roadmap. I do not know your starting point, your destination, what you are driving, or how much fuel you have. More importantly, I do not know your family. Every one of those variables matters. Given that all elements are different, your roadmap will also be different.

So rather than pretend there is a formula, I will explain how we approached this process. My hope is not that you copy it, but that you follow the logic and adapt it to your own situation.

Defining What "Family" Actually Means

The first step for us was defining what "family" actually means. In a generic sense, that is easy. In an estate and generational wealth context, it becomes far more complex. Ultimately, you must eventually narrow the definition to a very specific subset of individuals. In our case, we settled on direct descendants — the bloodline — but you will find that was not quite as straightforward as it sounds.

I am 81 as of this writing, so my family tree likely looks very different from yours if you are, say, 45. Both of our parents have long since passed, so my wife and I are either at the top or the bottom of the tree, depending on your perspective.

Combined, we have eight siblings. Not all are living. Some surviving spouses have passed, some have remarried, and some remain unmarried. Counting our own children, the next generation includes more than twenty people. Most are married, some have passed, some have remarried, and some are single.

The generation below that grows the number to well over one hundred individuals. All with the usual personalities, circumstances, opinions, and life paths. As far as I know, not a single one has any high-net-worth experience.

My wife is a naturalized citizen. As a result, much of her extended family resides outside the United States. Our family tree includes multiple races, religions, languages, political views, and orientations. We have biological as well as adopted children, including adopted grandchildren in the downline. Each sibling's branch has its own variations.

In short, our extended family probably looks a lot like yours ... Complex. Diverse. Human.

Which leads to the uncomfortable but necessary question: How do you rationally define who to include as heirs?

The Reality of Finite Resources

No matter the size of your pot of gold, it only stretches so far.

This process hinges entirely on your personal goals. If your goal is to spend everything before you die, then identifying heirs is largely an administrative exercise. Your estate planner simply needs names in case you depart before the last check bounces.

However, if your goals involve generational wealth, then scope matters. A great deal.

For example, if you have $10 million and 20 heirs, your legacy is not going to go very far. That is not harsh, it's math.

This brings up a related issue that people rarely think about in advance: **access versus ownership**.

Let's indulge in a brief fantasy. Suppose my wife and I were Tier 1+ UHNW. We own a condo on Maui, a ranch in Wyoming, and a flat in Paris. We are NetJets members allowing us to quietly move between residences while avoiding the unwashed masses.

I must admit, I am beginning to like this fantasy.

Now imagine we are in Paris for a few months and a relative calls and asks, "You're not using the Maui condo, can we stay there for our honeymoon?"

On the surface, that sounds reasonable. The property is vacant. No harm, right?

However, if you say yes to Mary or Pete, how do you say no to the other ninety-nine extended family members? Unfortunately, if you do not say no, over time your private assets will slowly become perceived as shared family assets.

For us, the answer is a hard and consistent "no."
Not unkind. Not dramatic. Just clear.

We may invite someone to join us as a guest.

- *They do not borrow properties.*
- *They do not "use" the aircraft.*
- *They do not assume access simply because something is idle.*

If you open that door, you will find it very difficult to close later. And if you do close it later, you will almost certainly earn lasting resentment. It is far better to set expectations up front than to attempt to restore boundaries in the future.

What is an Heir?

Before we discuss how we developed the heir pool, we need to be very clear about what the word "heir" means in our roadmap — *in our generational wealth context*.

This is not a traditional estate plan where money is distributed when you die and the structure dissolves. This is a Wealth Management Structure designed to continue indefinitely.

Heirs in this system are not waiting for a lump-sum inheritance. They are long-term beneficiaries of a structure that generates income over time. Distributions, if any, function more like dividends; they are not disbursements of principal.

The core wealth (the pot of gold) is intended to remain intact inside this structure. It is managed, invested, and used to produce ongoing income for current and future generations. This is the true definition of "**generational wealth**".

Non-bloodline individuals (such as spouses) may benefit indirectly during a beneficiary's lifetime, but they are not owners of the structure and they do not receive a traditional inheritance from it — no one does.

In simple terms

This is a generational wealth structure, not a one-time inheritance. The pot of gold stays inside the structure and keeps working. Heirs don't get the money itself — they receive dividends from what it produces.

Now that you understand what an heir actually is and how they benefit, the next step is deciding who qualifies for that role — and just as important, who does not.

Narrowing Our Heir Pool

Returning to the practical task of identifying heirs, we concluded that the most reasonable and manageable definition for our situation was direct bloodline descendants.

Based on our definition of an heir, we exclude:

- *Our siblings and their downlines*
- *Spouses within our downline (with legal considerations handled separately)*

That is not to say that we do not gift them, but they are not heirs.

We do include:

- *Legally adopted children and grandchildren*

We have not yet had to address adopted great-grandchildren, so that decision remains open for the future.

We also include great-grandchildren in situations where the bloodline parent has passed, and the surviving spouse has remarried. This can create stepsiblings who are not part of our bloodline. At present they are young, so it is not an immediate operational issue. However, it is something we will need to address in time.

Using these criteria narrowed our heir group to fewer than twenty individuals. Still a large number, but manageable relative to our goals and Tier level. We expect that number to grow as additional great-grandchildren arrive, but that will be offset somewhat as older heir pass.

The Integration Problem

Once we defined the heir pool, we faced the integration challenge — *onboarding*.

As I stressed in Phase 1, we have intentionally been very private. None of them had any real awareness of our financial situation.

Additionally, none were emotionally, educationally, or experientially prepared to deal with wealth of this nature.

This is not unusual. It is, in fact, the norm.

Step One: A Controlled Introduction

We began by inviting our two youngest daughters (stepsisters) to our home for an "emergency family meeting."

That selection was intentional. Both are intelligent and well educated with established careers. They represent the domestic and international sides of our family — they sit midway between their older siblings and our youngest grandchild — and they are very close to each other, allowing for private and candid discussion outside our presence.

When we invited them, they naturally asked what was going on. We politely dodged the question.

Establishing Confidentiality (Very Directly)

At the start of the meeting, we swore them to absolute secrecy.

- *No social media posts.*
- *No side conversations with siblings, spouses, in-laws, outlaws, children, or friends.*
- *Not now! Not later!*

We asked them to switch their phones and smart devices to airplane mode and leave them in another room.

We made the terms simple:

- *If you do not agree to complete confidentiality, we will not discuss this further. We can have dinner, enjoy the visit, and you can go home.*

Direct. Firm. No wiggle room.

We capped this with a statement — *"careless leaks could endanger your lives as well as ours"*. As expected, that raised eyebrows and generated immediate questions. My response was equally simple:
"If you stay through the weekend, you will understand."

They stayed. They agreed.

Controlled Disclosure (Not Full Transparency)

We then explained, in broad terms, that through long-term investments we generated substantial generational wealth.

They immediately asked two very reasonable questions:

- *How was it generated?*
- *How much are we talking about?*

We told them it was largely the result of investments, including crypto, which is only partially true, but the investment specifics are not important at this point, and that it was substantial.

- *We did not disclose amounts.*
    - *We did not discuss Tier ranges as they were unfamiliar with the Tier structure at this point.*
- *We did not disclose structural specifics.*

And we do not expect to do so for a very long time, if ever.

Too Much is Too Much

For onboarding purposes, it is enough that they understand the existence and seriousness of the structure. Exact numbers and exact structure are not required for responsible behavior. At some point we may tell them the Tier level, but not now.

Education Before Responsibility

We then gave each of them a pre-released copy of this book and asked them to read it before we continued any deeper discussion.

After dinner, we sent them to a nearby suites hotel so they could read, think, and talk privately. This was intentional. People process information better away from the immediate emotional gravity of the initial disclosure.

Their Actual Assignment (Very Specific)

The next morning, we reminded them of the need for security and confidentiality before we addressed why we had called them together.

We were not asking them to help design our financial structure.
That work had already been completed with our professional team.
Structures were in place. Funds were allocated.

Their task was limited to one very specific objective:
Help us develop a plan to onboard the remaining heirs.

We then told them who was included in the heir pool and how we arrived at our criteria. This naturally generated questions. We discussed those until they either agreed or, at minimum, understood that the selection criteria and specific heirs were not negotiable.

Why We Involved Them

Our reasoning was twofold.

First, this meeting itself was part of the onboarding process. Initially limiting it to two individuals was a manageable size.

Second, the heir group includes their older siblings as well as younger nieces and nephews. We wanted their generational and multicultural perspective in shaping a process that would be understandable to individuals at very different stages of life.

Our "Blind" Onboarding Philosophy

We made one principle very clear: the broader onboarding would occur largely "in the blind."

Like them, future heirs would:

- *Learn how HNW structures function*
- *Understand governance and expectations*
- *Be sworn to confidentiality*

Be given copies of this book.

Like them, they would not:

- *Know exact amounts*
- *Know structure or allocation details*

We are realistic. Leaks may happen.
However, you cannot leak what you do not know.
The blind onboarding approach supports both privacy and security.

Scope of the Plan We Requested

We also outlined the general elements we expected their proposed plan to address:

- *An "all-hands" gathering so everyone receives the same information at the same time*
    - *No "telephone" games*

List of what is to be covered

- *Scope of information to be revealed*
- *What is an heir, what is their role, what are the benefits*
- *Clear guidelines for handling questions, suggestions, and requests*
- *Onboarding of new spouses and future descendants*
- *Age-of-maturity considerations for younger heirs*
- *Prenuptial and postnuptial expectations*
- *Grounds for suspension or removal from the Heirs list*
- *Procedures for those unable to attend initial sessions*

We made it clear that other working groups may exist in the future — succession, education, philanthropy, or even a Family Office — but those topics were outside the scope of this specific assignment.

Final Thoughts

This is how we began our family onboarding process. Onboarding is not a technical exercise, it is a human one.

And humans, as you may have noticed, rarely fit neatly into spreadsheets.

I am intentionally excluding the detailed plan they ultimately developed. It is highly specific to our family, personalities, and circumstances.

It is important that you create your own process rather than attempt to copy someone else's.

Practical Cautions — A Do-Not List

Before you begin your own onboarding process, it may be helpful to understand a few approaches we strongly recommend avoiding. These are based on human nature, not financial theory.

Do not begin with a large "all-hands" family meeting.

Group settings amplify emotion, speculation, misunderstanding, and potentially grandstanding that can easily derail the process. Individuals will grasp the subjects at different rates, rumors and doubts can emerge and the audience can quickly spiral into fear, excitement, entitlement, or conflict before any structure is understood. Smaller, carefully selected introductions are far more stable.

Our strategy for onboarding two individuals early was in part so that these two could "read the crowd" (manage the floor) and help us pace the all-hands meeting to avoid these types of problems.

If your heir pool is larger, you may want to have a second stage introduction to a group of 4 or 5 additional heirs so that they will be better able to manage the floor during the all -hands meeting. Find or manufacture a reason for a second working group to engage these second-round heirs. Follow the same process to introduce them to the new world.

Do not assume age equals readiness.

The oldest heir is not automatically the most discreet, emotionally stable, or capable of processing sensitive information. Maturity, temperament, and judgment matter far more than birth order. A natural leader or a respected member is far better.

Do not select your initial onboarding group based on favoritism or convenience.

This is a strategic working group, not a social circle. You do not want a sycophant in this group. Choosing the wrong initial participants can create long-term internal divisions that are difficult to repair.

Do not disclose financial amounts early.

… and <u>never</u> to the entire group.

Exact numbers could overwhelm, distract, and distort behavior. At early stages, understanding responsibility and structure is far more important than knowing the size of the assets.

Do not minimize the importance of privacy and security.

What feels like harmless sharing with one family member can become permanent exposure once spoken, posted, or casually repeated. Privacy expectations must be explicit, direct, and non-negotiable from the beginning.

Even with the best intentions, information will leak; however, they cannot leak what they do not know.

Do not assume confidentiality will occur naturally.

It will not. Even intelligent and well-meaning family members may share information unintentionally unless expectations are clearly stated in advance.

Do not over-explain the structure too early.

Newly informed heirs are often emotionally processing the reality of wealth itself. Excessive technical detail at this stage can create confusion rather than clarity.

Do not delay onboarding indefinitely out of discomfort.

Avoidance may feel easier in the short term, but it increases long-term risk. If something unexpected occurs, unprepared heirs may be forced to make critical decisions without context or guidance.

Do not allow access to assets to precede education and expectations.

Access without understanding can permanently alter family dynamics and individual behavior in ways that are difficult to reverse.

Do not forget that this is a human process, not merely a financial one.

Be sensitive, fear, excitement, insecurity, and curiosity will all be present, whether spoken or not. Planning for these reactions is just as important as planning the legal and financial structure.

Carefully handled, onboarding can create alignment, stability, long-term stewardship and help stimulate the group. Handled casually, it can unintentionally create confusion, entitlement, and internal conflict that persists for generations.

Phase 8: Family Alignment

Goal

Ensure your wealth does not destroy the people you love.

Reason

Providing access and/or control of substantial wealth when you are unprepared is detrimental to the long-term survival of the legacy you have created, but it is also dangerous for the well-being of the unprepared individual.

This phase gets personal. It cannot be avoided. You must honestly and fairly evaluate individual heirs to assess their preparedness to deal with potentially large sums of money and to identify future leaders/managers of the wealth you have accumulated. This is not a punitive process but an educational exercise. Few will be prepared to assume the responsibilities, but most will be able to step up. As the leader, mentorship is your responsibility. It is your responsibility to not only identify, but to guide and educate or arrange education to grow their capabilities.

Action

This Phase Is Not Immediate (Don't Rush It)

You should not attempt family alignment until:

- *Your offshore trust/LLCs are established*
- *Your banking layers are operating*
- *Your domestic privacy structure is in place*
- *Your own life is stabilized and private*
- *You have gone through Phases 1–7 without leaks*
- *You have onboarded your heirs*

Only then do you begin preparing heirs.

Attempting these conversations early:

- *Creates expectation and entitlement*
- *Increases risk of leaks*
- *Gives heirs influence before your structure is locked down*
- *Makes you vulnerable to emotional pressure*

This phase is about future stewardship, not present involvement.

I Have No Potential Leader to Follow Me

If your heir pool is small or young, there may not be an individual to logically follow you to lead the group. If no individual is capable or of age, you should work with your advisory team to develop a plan to bridge the gap.

Clarify Your Wealth Philosophy ("The Family Operating System")

Beyond documents … distributions … and trusts

Your heirs must understand your philosophy of wealth.

This is not a legal document — it's the **"owner's manual" for your money.**

Your Wealth Philosophy Should Cover

- *Money is a tool, not an identity.*
- *Opportunity support vs. lifestyle support.*
  "We help you build ladders, not buy hammocks."
- *Your definition of meaningful work and contribution.*
- *How you evaluate requests for help.*
- *Expectations for stewardship, privacy, and personal behavior.*
- *Reasons for suspension or removal of heirs*

Deliverable

A 1-3 page plain-language "Wealth Manifesto" that each adult heir signs.

Opportunity Support, Not An Endless ATM

This must be hammered into their bones.

Opportunity Support Equals

Funding education, training, business starts, down payments (with guardrails), or emergency medical needs.

NOT Supported

Lifestyle upgrades, impulsive purchases, debt bailouts, or "just because" requests.

You may choose to codify this through:

- *Trust distribution rules*
- *Family handbook*
- *Family meetings*
- *A private written agreement (heirs sign)*

This is where generational disasters are prevented.

Written Family Rules for Requesting Money

Structure prevents resentment and manipulation.

Typical Rules (customizable)

1. Requests must be written, not verbal.
2. Requests must explain the goal, not just the item.
3. "How will this change your life in 10 years?" must be answered.
4. If the trust funds it, the heir must match a percentage (skin in the game).
   a. The heir, not the heir's parent, spouse, or other

5. No spouse or partner speaks for an heir.
6. Requests are reviewed quarterly, not on demand.
7. Small emergency funds exist, but capped and monitored.

Begin Soft-Disclosure to Select Heirs (Need-to-Know Only)

Do not dump the entire financial picture on them. Reveal **exactly enough** so they understand their coming responsibilities.

Level 1 — Outline Only

- *What money means, why privacy matters, why trusts exist.*
- *No numbers.*
- *Read this Roadmap.*

Level 2 — Structural Overview

Explain:

- *There is an offshore layer (CIT or equivalent)*
- *There are domestic LLCs*
- *There is multi-level asset protection*

No dollar amounts.

Level 3 — Limited Numbers

- *Only for heirs likely to serve as future trustees or managers.*
- *Only the Tier level at this time.*
- ***Never disclose the full picture to everyone.***

You keep the "master key" private.

Evaluate Each Heir Honestly (Quietly)

This is not about fairness — it's about protecting them from themselves.

Privately Assess

- *Their maturity*
- *Their addictions or vulnerability to relationships*
- *Their spending patterns*
- *Their effort to learn more about wealth management*
- *Their emotional stability*
- *Their ability to keep secrets*
- *Their capacity to manage money responsibly*

This Dictates

- *Their distribution level*
- *Whether they receive money or access to money*
- *Whether you use staggered ages vs. milestone-based releases*
- *Whether they get voting shares or non-voting shares in the domestic entities*
- *Whether their organizational responsibilities are elevated*

Assign Roles: Who Becomes What?

You need to decide:

- *Future trustee(s)*
- *Business managers for domestic LLCs*
- *Family council members*
- *Beneficiaries vs. contributors*

Most families incorrectly give heirs decision power.

Heirs Benefit, Professionals Manage

For the truly competent heir, you will want to gradually integrate them into:

- *Annual reviews*
- *Limited decision authority*
- *Future leadership training*

Don't assume "the oldest" should lead anything.

Professional Background Checks

As part of formal governance practices, most established Family Offices periodically conduct structured risk reviews — which can include background checks — on heirs, spouses, and individuals who could materially affect the family's financial structure.

This mirrors practices used by financial institutions and other organizations responsible for safeguarding significant assets. This is not personal distrust; it is prudent risk management.

When substantial capital, complex structures, and long-term stewardship are involved, responsible oversight becomes part of the system itself.

Whether and how to implement such reviews is a governance decision. It should be discussed with your professional advisory team and aligned with your family's values, privacy standards, and long-term objectives.

The level of review should reflect the heir's level of involvement and consequently risk to the organization. Are they simply receiving dividend distributions, a LLC Manager, a Trustee, or are they actively involved in upper-level management of the Wealth Management Structure, meeting with the advisory team, bankers, assisting in investment decisions, etc. Regardless of current level, are they scheduled to move up the management level.

Any discussion of professional background reviews or similar governance safeguards should be handled in consultation with qualified legal counsel. This roadmap is intentionally limited to strategic planning and does not provide investigative guidance, which is the proper domain of legal and fiduciary advisors.

Build A "Family Handbook" (Short, Practical)

This is NOT legalese.

This is the "owner's manual" for the family.

Chapters usually include

- *The family wealth philosophy*
- *Rules for money requests*
- *Expectations about privacy*
- *Trust distribution principles*
- *Behavioral expectations*
- *Emergency protocols*
- *How disputes are handled*
- *Behavioral guidelines for heirs*
- *Who to contact if something happens to you*

This book prevents most future chaos.

Conduct the First Private Family Meeting

This will be the first meeting following the initial onboarding process meeting.

A good first meeting:

- *Does not disclose wealth numbers.*

61

- *Introduces values, privacy, and basic structure.*
- *Allows heirs to ask safe questions.*
- *Establishes that this is a process, not a lecture.*
- *Sets the tone:*
  "You are responsible to the family, not entitled from it."
  "Your personal conduct reflects on the family and can affect your status as an heir."

If you don't control the narrative early, they'll invent one.

Rehearse Scenarios (Quietly with advisors)

What if

- *An heir divorces?*
- *An heir develops addiction?*
- *An heir has serious legal issues?*
- *A spouse begins manipulating?*
- *There is a dispute between heirs?*
- *There's a lawsuit?*
- *One heir is responsible and the others aren't?*
- *A grandchild needs support independently of their parents?*

Your team helps you build the guardrails before a storm hits.

High-net-worth families who don't rehearse scenarios can break when the first crisis comes.

Integrate with Estate Documents But Keep Heirs Away

Your trust documents will reflect:

- *The family operating system*
- *The distribution rules*

- *Incentive structures*
- *Milestone qualifications*
- *Emergency exceptions*
- *Trustee oversight*

But Remember

Your heirs are beneficiaries; not co-authors, they do not negotiate your trust language.

Phase 8 Ends When

You have prepared your heirs emotionally, structurally, and contractually to handle responsibility — not entitlement.

- *You have a written wealth philosophy / manifesto.*
- *You have communicated / enforced the "opportunity support vs. ATM" rule.*
- *You documented rules for requesting money.*
- *You privately evaluated each heir's strengths and weaknesses.*
- *You assigned future roles (even if tentative).*
- *You created a simple Family Handbook.*
- *You held the first structured family meeting.*
- *Your advisors have rehearsed multiple scenarios with you.*
- *You firmly control the narrative.*

When this phase is complete, your heirs will be prepared — emotionally and structurally — to receive wealth without being ruined by it.

Mr Timothy J Griswold

Phase 9: Living The Plan

Goal

Operate your life and wealth-structure at a steady, disciplined pace so it remains invisible, protected, functional, and stress-free.

This phase is about **maintenance**, not building. You now live inside your system — you don't rebuild it every year.

Reason

Most sudden-wealth failures happen after the structure is built.
People relax, talk too much, get sloppy, or let emotions override discipline.

This phase prevents:

- *Leaks*
- *Lifestyle creep*
- *Impulse giving*
- *Recklessness*
- *Sabotage by spouses, relatives, or advisors*
- *Panic reactions during market swings*
- *Slow decay of an otherwise perfect plan*

This is the phase where you prove you can keep what you built.

Actions

Maintain Operational Silence (Forever)

- *Never discuss your wealth, structure, accounts, or plans with anyone outside your professional team.*

- *Never disclose your offshore elements to anyone except your attorneys.*
- *Never post about money, luxury, or major purchases on social media.*
- *Never tell family members "how much" is in the system. They get information on a need-to-know basis only.*

Silence is the cheapest form of insurance ever invented.

Live Below the Radar

- *If you upgrade your home, keep it modest from the street.*
- *If you buy cars, buy quality — not spectacle.*
- *If you travel, do so quietly.*
- *If you spend, use your domestic LLCs so purchases are not tied to your personal name.*

The fewer signals you send, the fewer threats you attract.

Perform Annual System Maintenance

Once a year (your "Wealth Maintenance Day"):

- *Meet with your attorney to confirm trust compliance, distributions, and succession.*
- *Meet with your CPA to confirm filings and tax alignment.*
- *Ensure your offshore trustee delivers required reports.*
- *Audit each LLC (domestic and offshore) for compliance, renewals, and proper usage.*
- *Review status of heirs (behavior, stability, relationships, employment).*
- *Check security (physical, digital, financial).*
- *Update beneficiary lists if needed.*

This is not reinvention — this is **preventative maintenance**.

Keep Your Lifestyle Scaled to Your Plan

Your plan determines:

- *Your home*
- *Your travel*
- *Your charitable activity*
- *Your hobbies*
- *Your risk tolerance*
- *Your exposure*

Not the other way around.

If your lifestyle grows faster than your system, you're doing it wrong.

Give and Support Intentionally (Not Emotionally):

- *Support family through opportunity, not ATM cash.*
- *Fund education, not consumption.*
- *Fund skill-building, not lifestyle inflation.*
- *Help with launchpads, not lifelong allowances.*
- *Give to charities only after professional due diligence.*

You are **not an ATM** and must never feel like one.

Use Professionals, Not Friends

- *Keep your advisor relationships clean, contractual, and unemotional.*
- *Never let a "friend" do your legal work, accounting, PI work, or investing.*
- *Replace professionals who get sloppy, arrogant, or dismissive.*
- *Require written explanations for all recommendations.*
- *If someone objects to documentation, they're fired.*

Friendship does not belong in your command structure.

Update Your Heir Intelligence Files

Every 2–3 years

- *Run updates on spouses, partners, and key associates of each heir.*
- *Update psychological and behavioral observations (trends matter).*
- *Watch for addiction, debt, destructive relationships, or instability.*
- *Update your trustee's guidance memo accordingly.*

Your heirs evolve — so must your intelligence.

Prepare for Life Shocks

Because they will happen.

Have protocols for:

- *Divorce*
- *Unexpected death*
- *Medical crisis*
- *Lawsuits*
- *Major economic downturns*
- *Family conflict*
- *New heirs (marriage, children)*
- *Inherited responsibility (death of spouse or parent)*

The structure you built in Phases 1–8 allows you to:

Respond calmly, legally, and with zero panic.

Continually Reaffirm Your Endgame

Every year, revisit:

- *Your lifestyle goals*
- *Your legacy goals*
- *Your risk comfort*
- *Your trust instructions*
- *Which heirs are ready, and which are not*

Your wealth plan is a living organism — small adjustments keep it healthy.

Do Not

- *Do not brag, disclose, or hint at your wealth.*
- *Do not let heirs treat you like a funding source.*
- *Do not let lifestyle creep exceed your plan.*
- *Do not allow advisors to act without written instruction.*
- *Do not skip maintenance years.*
- *Do not add complexity you don't understand.*
- *Do not relax your discipline. Wealth is easiest to lose when you think it's permanent.*

Phase 9 Ends When

This phase NEVER ENDS.

Appendices

Mr Timothy J Griswold

A: Wealth Manager vs. Private Bank

What You Must Know Before You Choose

This is one of the most misunderstood areas of sudden wealth — and one of the easiest places to be misled. Most people assume "wealth manager" and "private bank" mean the same thing.

They do not.

They are fundamentally different animals. They have different incentives, different responsibilities, and different levels of accountability. Choosing the wrong one can sabotage everything you built in Phases 1–9.

Wealth Managers

What They Are

A wealth manager is usually:

- *An employee at a brokerage*
- *A financial advisor at a brand-name investment house*
- *A salesperson with licenses to sell investment products*
- *Someone whose compensation is tied to assets managed, products sold, or commissions*

They may call themselves:

- *"Private Wealth Advisor"*
- *"Portfolio Manager"*
- *"Retirement Specialist"*
- *"Family Office Advisor"*
- *"Investment Consultant"*

Titles mean nothing.

Certification means nothing.

Most are product distributors, not fiduciaries.

What Wealth Managers Actually Do

Typical services include:

- *Investment allocation*
- *Selling annuities, packaged products, structured notes*
- *Retirement projections*
- *Basic estate planning referrals*
- *General financial planning*
- *Tax-loss harvesting at year-end*

They rarely coordinate with attorneys, trustees, CPAs, or offshore structures.

They operate in a **domestic bubble**.

Limitations / Risks

- *They want custody of your money so they can charge fees*
- *They do not protect assets — they only invest them*
- *They usually have no offshore expertise*
- *They often do NOT understand Cook Islands, Nevis, Liechtenstein, or Singapore structures*
- *They push the firm's preferred products (conflict of interest)*
- *They default to U.S.-based custody (bad for privacy and protection)*
- *They have no legal authority or infrastructure to handle complex wealth systems*

Bottom Line

A wealth manager is optional, and potentially dangerous if used improperly.

Private Banks

Private banks provide a comprehensive, personalized financial service tailored to high-net-worth individuals and often their businesses. They go far beyond standard banking by offering a dedicated private banker who acts as a single point of contact for all financial matters.

Core Services

- *Personalized Wealth Management: Customized investment strategies, portfolio management, and asset allocation based on the client's goals, risk tolerance, and time horizon.*
- *Comprehensive Financial Planning: Can include retirement planning, estate and succession planning, tax optimization, and trust services to preserve wealth across generations.*
- *Tailored Lending & Credit Solutions: Jumbo mortgages, secured loans using assets (like real estate or portfolios), and flexible credit lines with favorable terms.*
- *Exclusive Investment Access: Entry to private equity, hedge funds, venture capital, alternative investments, and other opportunities not available to retail investors.*
- *Enhanced Banking Features: Includes premium accounts with higher interest rates, fee waivers, optimized interest rates, and priority service on standard banking products like checking and savings.*
- *Concierge & Lifestyle Services: Many private banks offer lifestyle management, such as travel planning, event coordination, and luxury asset management.*
- *Secure Offshore Custody: for things like precious metals.*

They are not product salespeople.

They are infrastructure.

Key Differentiators

- ***Dedicated Relationship Manager:*** *Clients have a personal banker who understands their full financial picture and handles everything from bill payments to complex investments.*
- ***High Minimums & Fees:*** *Typically requires significant assets (often $1 million or more) and charges fees based on assets under management (AUM), which can include management fees, transaction costs, and service charges.*
- ***Privacy & Security:*** *Ensures strict confidentiality and advanced security for sensitive financial information.*
- ***One-Stop Financial Hub:*** *Integrates banking, investment, tax, and estate planning under a single roof, simplifying complex financial management.*
- ***Maintain the "financial heartbeat" of your entire system***

Strengths

- *They know how to work with Cook Islands trustees*
- *They handle Nevis LLC structures without flinching*
- *They understand privacy, asset protection, and cross-border requirements*
- *They provide institutional-level security*
- *They are not shocked by large balances or global activity*
- *Their risk teams protect YOU as much as themselves*

Bottom Line

A private bank is the correct financial engine for the structure you built in this manual.

Which One Do You Need?

If you have domestic-only assets and want simple investing, NOT the structure outlined in this plan:

- *A wealth manager is sufficient*

If you have offshore structures, multi-jurisdiction assets, and a long-term protection plan:

- *You need a private bank.*

If your net worth is Tier 4:

- *A hybrid approach is fine.*

If your net worth is Tier 3 - 1+:

- *You need a fully integrated private banking relationship.*

If your net worth is Tier 1 or Tier 1+ private banks are critical.
You should have:

- *One domestic private bank*
- *One offshore private bank*
- *One private investment office* (optional)*
- ***No retail wealth managers whatsoever***

*A **Private Investment Office**, in this context, refers to a dedicated internal or semi-internal team (or outsourced equivalent) focused on coordinating investments, managers, reporting, and strategic allocation across multiple asset classes. It is not a retail advisory relationship, but a governance-level investment coordination function.

Recommendation Summary

Wealth Manager

Use only if:

- *You want someone to manage a portion of your portfolio*
- *You keep them on a short leash*
- *You do NOT give them custody of your core assets*
- *They do NOT interact with your offshore structure*

Private Bank

Use for

- *Primary custody*
- *Multi-currency accounts*
- *Integration with your trust/LLCs*
- *Institutional security*
- *Compliant international transfers*
- *Wealth longevity*
- *Serious estate planning*

Clear Rule

Your **private bank is the engine.**

Your **structure is the body armor.**

Your **advisors are the command staff.**

Your **wealth manager, if any, is scenery.**

Incorporating a wealth manager WILL complicate your tax and compliance issues.

B: The Siren Song of DIY Investing

At some point, every newly wealthy person thinks:

"Why don't I just do this myself?"
I see it on YouTube, all I need are three index funds. Easy and Cheap.

Here's the truth

Yes — you can DIY.

For simple, domestic, retirement-level money, that's perfectly fine. However, DIY does not fit in a structured wealth management system. **DIY breaks down** the moment you enter the world of generational wealth; that is what this manual is preparing you for.

Here's Why

DIY Means "YOU Are the Weakest Link"

One mistake — even a small one — can:

- *Break compliance rules*
- *Violate your trust's terms*
- *Create a taxable event*
- *Expose assets during a lawsuit*
- *Collapse the protection structure*
- *Trigger international reporting errors*

YouTube teaches you how to pick funds, but you're maintaining a **multi-jurisdictional system** with complex legal, tax, and banking consequences.

YouTube does not prepare you for that.

DIY Gives You Zero Leverage Power

When your assets sit in a DIY brokerage account:

- *You cannot obtain low-interest credit facilities*
- *You cannot borrow against your portfolio at institutional rates*
- *You cannot access multi-currency lending*
- *You cannot secure bridge financing for real estate*
- *You cannot execute complex transactions quickly*
- *You cannot get priority settlement or wire support*

DIY is **custody without leverage**.

A private bank is **custody with power.**

DIY Has No Institutional Protection Layer

When you manage your own money:

- *You are the fraud-detection team*
- *You are the compliance department*
- *You are the cybersecurity staff*
- *You are the wire-approval system*
- *You are the risk officer*

Almost anything you do with your stocks will generate a tax event. Private banks have teams of professionals whose full-time job is to prevent:

- *Unnecessary taxes*
- *Fraud*
- *Identity theft*
- *Errors*
- *Sanctions violations*
- *Cyber attacks*

A DIY investor has none of that.

DIY Cannot Integrate With an Offshore Trust

Brokerages will not open accounts for:

- *Cook Islands trusts*
- *Nevis LLCs owned by offshore trusts*
- *Liechtenstein foundations*
- *Singapore trust structures*

Even if they *could,* they won't because a nonprofessional manager increases their risk.

This is why DIY becomes **a structural failure**, not just a financial one.

DIY Limits Opportunities to Only "Retail Products"

The entire world of:

- *Institutional funds*
- *Private credit*
- *Real estate syndicates*
- *Structured lending*
- *Private secondary markets*
- *Specialized multi-currency products*
- *Institutional-level liquidity services*

… are closed to DIY portfolios.

A private bank opens doors.

DIY leaves you standing on the sidewalk outside.

DIY Creates Psychological Traps

When you push the "buy" and "sell" buttons:

- *Fear drives decisions*
- *FOMO drives decisions*
- *Market noise drives decisions*
- *Emotion overrides discipline*

Professionals don't react to dramatic media stories. Retail investors do.

That's why retail consistently underperforms institutional management by wide margins over time.

DIY — Not for Wealth Preservation

This manual is about becoming — **Invisible. Protected. Unreachable. Multi-layered. Bulletproof.**

DIY can buy the S&P 500.

DIY cannot:

- *Shield assets from predatory lawsuits*
- *Operate inside a Cook Islands system*
- *Interface with offshore trustees*
- *Coordinate cross-border banking*
- *Maintain privacy across jurisdictions*
- *Execute multi-layer estate strategies*
- *Support a dynasty or multi-generation legacy*

DIY is "**building a tent.**"

Private banking is "**building a fortress.**"

Bottom Line

DIY may look cheaper.
It may feel familiar.
It may give you a feeling of control.

But it is not compatible with generational wealth:

- *Offshore structures*
- *Serious asset protection*
- *Privacy*
- *Leverage*

- *Multi-jurisdiction systems*
- *Legacy planning*
- *Professional coordination*
- *Long-term security*

A private bank isn't there to "beat the market."

It's there to **protect the structure**, empower you globally, and give your wealth a professional operating system.

DIY as a Hobby

You are rich now so you might want to develop a new hobby. If you want to play in the financial markets, DIY might be fun. Take **a small piece** of gold and play. Don't risk the whole pot.

YouTube can teach you how to invest. It cannot teach you how to preserve wealth across generations. If you work at it, you might well beat the pros from time to time.

Remember, while DIY is for accumulation, private banking is for preservation.

C: Governance Models

Governance Matters More Than Documents

Effective governance is the backbone of every durable wealth structure. Legal documents create authority, but governance determines how authority is exercised, by whom, and under what constraints. Most long-term failures in wealthy families trace back not to flawed trusts but flawed governance.

Governance Decision-Making Models

Grantor-Led

The grantor (that is you) retains key powers during their lifetime. Offers speed and clarity but requires a succession plan.

Committee-Led

A small group (trusted advisors, senior family members) executes major decisions. Useful for continuity and checks / balances.

Protector-Led

A Protector is an independent individual or entity appointed within certain trust structures to provide an additional layer of oversight, with limited powers defined in the trust documents (such as replacing trustees or approving specific actions). The Protector's role is governance-focused, not operational.

The trust protector has authority to override, remove, or replace trustees. Ideal for families prioritizing stability and long-term control.

Beneficiary-Informed vs. Beneficiary-Blind:

- *Informed: Beneficiaries understand structures and expectations.*
- *Blind: Beneficiaries know little to avoid entitlement. Works only if governance is strong.*

Roles and Authorities

Trustee

Administers the trust, manages assets, and executes distributions.

Co-Trustees

Divide powers across individuals or entities to reduce risk.

Distribution Committee

Guides or approves distribution decisions, reinforcing consistency.

Trust Protector

A non-fiduciary role with limited but powerful oversight functions.

Special-Purpose Fiduciaries

Experts brought in for narrow duties (e.g., investments, real estate, operating businesses).

Trust Protector Architecture

A modern trust should include a clearly defined protector system.

Core Powers:

- *Remove / replace trustees*
- *Veto distributions*
- *Amend administrative provisions*
- *Resolve deadlocks*
- *Modify governing law or situs (where appropriate)*

Protector Limits

Powers should be strong but not unlimited. Excessive authority risks tax issues or fiduciary reclassification.

Succession of Protectors

Define a successor hierarchy, selection rules, and removal processes.

Checks & Balances

- *Split roles (no concentration of power)*
- *Require multi-signature approvals for major actions*
- *Build redundancy to prevent single points of failure*
- *Require regular reporting to the protector*

Keeping Beneficiaries Safe, but Not Spoiled

Frameworks should

- *Protect from self-inflicted harm*
- *Encourage responsibility*
- *Avoid unconditional access*
- *Reward productive behavior while shielding from entitlement*

Governance Failure Modes

- *Trustee burnout or incompetence*
- *No successor plan*
- *Beneficiaries gaining too much information too early*
- *Overreliance on a single advisor*
- *Conflicts between trust language and intended governance*

D: Family Offices

What is a Family Office

A Family Office (FO) is the "operating system" for long-term wealth. It does not replace a wealth manager, an investment advisor, a private bank, or any of the specialized functions defined in Phases 1–9. Instead, **its core purpose is to coordinate all of them**.

The FO protects, manages, reports, and executes across every domain of family life—financial, legal, operational, administrative, and, when necessary, personal. Wealth creates complexity, and complexity left unmanaged becomes risk. Governance will happen one way or another; the only question is whether it will be intentional or accidental.

Proactive FO management ensures that required functions occur on time and in the right way: tax filings, reporting, distributions, entity maintenance, compliance, documentation, asset monitoring, and long-term stability. Without this coordination, the family is left hoping that dozens of independent advisors will magically align. Experience shows they will not.

A well-designed FO will allow a family to sleep at night.

There are many flavors of Family Offices appropriate for different wealth levels, personalities, and goals. Much like with a company, you may choose to manage the FO yourself or hire a person to manage the day-to-day operations. The choice is yours, it will depend on your desire, skills, and possibly the Tier level. Obviously, Tier 1 and 1+, will require progressively more time than Tier 3. It is also possible that you initially take a hands-on approach but transition to a professional manager as you grow more comfortable with the overall operation.

This appendix is not intended to be a comprehensive FO construction manual—there are excellent books and highly specialized professionals for that. Instead, this appendix introduces the FO concept, outlines the major types, and shows how they might integrate with your governance system. The intention is to make you aware of these structures so you can discuss the options with your advisory team to determine what structure might best fits your circumstances.

Why Wealthy Families Build FOs:

- *Centralization*
- *Accountability*
- *Reduced leakage*
- *Privacy and security*
- *Long-term continuity*

Types of FOs

- *Virtual FO*
  Entirely outsourced; ideal for transition phases.
- *Fractional FO*
  Part-time CFO/COO roles sourced from external providers.
- *Multi-Family Office (MFO)*
  Shared infrastructure with individualized services.
- *Single Family Office (SFO)*
  Fully internalized structure; highest control, highest cost.

Core FO Functions

- *Governance support*
- *Accounting & reporting*
- *Cash flow management*
- *Legal coordination (trusts, entities, estate)*
- *Investment oversight*
- *Insurance & risk management*
- *Security (cyber + physical)*
- *Real estate oversight*
- *Special projects and major transactions*

Organizational Models

- ***Lean Model***
  1–3 internal staff leveraging outsourced specialists.
- ***Balanced Model***
  Core internal team with external augmentation.
- ***Integrated Model***
  Fully built SFO with in-house investment, accounting, and security teams.

Operational Governance

Key Interactions

- *Trustees receive reporting from the FO*
- *Protectors audit FO activities*
- *Committees rely on FO for data and execution*

This creates a loop of authority, oversight, and execution.

Security & Privacy Framework

- *Controlled communications*
- *Secure data storage*
- *Discreet financial behavior*
- *No unnecessary public filings*
- *Compartmentalization of sensitive information*

Building a Lightweight SFO

A practical model that avoids the typical $2–4M/year FO burn rate.

Core Components

- *Outsourced investment management*
- *Internal FO Director (part-time or fractional)*
- *External CPA + legal team*
- *Security consultant on retainer*
- *Project-based specialists*

Integration Models

- ***Vertical Integration***
  FO controls and coordinates everything from trusts to real estate.
- ***Modular Integration***
  FO manages certain domains while specialized outside firms handle the rest.

Family Office Lifecycle

Work with your core professional team to understand how a FO might fit your situation and what type of FO would work best. The structure and scope may change over time as your situation matures.

- ***Stage 1: Stabilization***
  Create structure, documentation, and reporting.
- ***Stage 2: Mature Operation***
  Predictable processes, reliable governance, annual reviews.
- ***Stage 3: Succession***
  Transition authority gradually while preserving original intent.

E: Annual Reviews

This appendix provides practical, high-level checklists to ensure that all structures described in the manual are implemented, maintained, and reviewed on a predictable schedule. It is not a substitute for professional guidance; it simply helps to ensures that nothing critical slips through the cracks.

Initial Implementation Checklist

- *Entity formation verified and documented*
- *Trusts executed and funded*
- *Banking, brokerage, and custody accounts aligned with structure*
- *Insurance policies reviewed and updated*
- *Security protocols confirmed*
- *Tax planning coordinated with all advisors*

Annual Review Checklist

- *Trust protector meeting*
- *Trustee annual report*
- *Investment performance oversight*
- *Insurance review*
- *Legal and tax updates*
- *Risk and security audit*

Event-Driven Checklist

- *Major liquidity event*
- *Asset sale or acquisition*
- *Change in family circumstances*
- *Change in residency or jurisdiction*

F: Advisor Selection

This appendix outlines the high-level framework for choosing, managing, and replacing key advisors. It does not attempt to teach the technical skills needed to evaluate professionals; instead, it clarifies the structural expectations.

Core Advisor Categories

- *Estate and tax attorneys*
- *CPA and accounting team*
- *Investment advisor(s)*
- *Insurance / risk specialists*
- *FO Director or equivalent coordinator*
- *Security and Privacy consultants*

Selection Criteria (High-Level)

- *Competence and specialization*
- *Transparency and communication*
- *Alignment with long-term goals*
- *Absence of conflicts*
- *Cost clarity*

Oversight Expectations

- *Scheduled reporting*
- *Performance measurement*
- *Documentation standards*
- *Coordination with other advisors*

Replacement Triggers

- *Misalignment of goals*
- *Performance issues*
- *Lack of responsiveness*
- *Governance conflicts*

G: Continuity Protocols

A structured way to ensure all documents are catalogued, securely stored, and accessible to those who require them.

Core Document Categories

- *Trusts and amendments*
- *Wills and powers of attorney*
- *Entity formation documents*
- *Banking and brokerage records*
- *Insurance policies*
- *Real estate documents*
- *Security and access records*

Storage Framework

- *Physical originals (vault or safe storage)*
- *Digital duplicates (encrypted)*
- *FO-level indexing*
- *Access rights and restrictions*

Continuity Protocols

- *Who receives what documents upon incapacity or death*
- *Protector and trustee notification sequences*
- *Advisor's activation order*

A Closing Note

At this point, you may feel overwhelmed.

Relax, take a breath; you got this!

What you have in your hand is a series of nine phases structured to gradually increase your involvement and your knowledge. As you build from one phase to the next you will see your progress along the way.

They show you when to bring in professional help, and what specific help you will need. Through this process, I have given you the basic language and structural elements that will allow you to communicate about subjects that might otherwise feel intimidating.

Use this book is your "*navigator*" it lays out what you need to begin organizing your new life. If at any point you start feeling lost or overwhelmed, come back to this roadmap. It will help you reorient so that you can proceed.

There are, of course, two alternatives. You could simply ignore everything and spend until the money is gone. Or you could turn total control over to an individual or organization and hope for the best. I don't know about you, but for me, neither of those alternatives are acceptable.

This is my roadmap. I designed it to meet my goal:
Living an invisible, bulletproof life that allows me to sleep at night.

Use it as your starting roadmap. Define your goal then adapt this material to accomplish it.

Thank you for taking the time and trusting me enough to listen. I wish you and your family a great new life of abundance.

About the Author

Tim Griswold is an engineer with an MBA. He specializes in developing executable solutions to complex problems. He writes about strategy, decision-making, and the challenges that arise as life circumstances change.

His work focuses on helping individuals and companies navigate complex transitions with discipline and clarity.

His memoir, *From Shasta to Shanghai,* offers a broader look at the experiences that shaped his perspective.

He lives in the United States.

Bulk order inquiries:

orders@tgpubs.com

Reader comments are welcome:

readers@tgpubs.com

Made in United States
North Haven, CT
04 November 2026

21769298R00065